ALL ABOUT ME

My Growing Body

CARYN JENNER

W

FRANKLIN WATTS

LONDON • SYDNEY

Franklin Watts
338 Euston Road
London NW1 3BH

Franklin Watts Australia
Level 17/207 Kent Street
Sydney, NSW 2000

Series editor: Sarah Peutrill
Art director: Jonathan Hair
Design: Rawshock design
Picture researcher: Kathy Lockley
Illustrations: John Alston
Consultant: Dr T K Holmes

Dewey number: 612.6'5

ISBN 978 1 4451 2976 1

Printed in China

Franklin Watts is a division of
Hachette Children's Books, an
Hachette UK company.
www.hachette.co.uk

CONTENTS

Our life cycle 6

How your body grows 8

Babies 10

Toddlers 12

Early childhood 14

Middle years 16

Teenage years 18

From girls to women 20

From boys to men 22

An adult 24

Being you 26

Glossary 28

Further information 29

Index 30

(Words in **bold** are in the glossary on page 28.)

What is always changing but we hardly ever notice? It's us! We are born and we grow from children into **adults**, then we may have our own children. We keep growing older and in the end, we die. These changes are the **life cycle** of a **human being**.

GROWING

When you are a child you grow a lot. You can see this when your feet get too big for your shoes or when you look at photos of when you were younger. Childhood is the years between when you are born and when you have finished growing and can look after yourself, usually at about the age of 18. Then you are an adult, but you still continue to change.

These pictures show some of the stages of the human life cycle.

Baby

Toddler

Early childhood

EVERYONE IS DIFFERENT

Some things about you are the same as some other people; the colour of your eyes or hair for example, or that you like swimming or dancing. But no one else in the entire world is exactly like you. You have your own look and **personality**. You even grow and change a little differently to everyone else. There are many different people in the world, and each of us is **unique**.

Nowadays, people in countries like the United Kingdom often live to age 80 or older. But 200 years ago, people were only expected to live to age 40.

Middle childhood

Teenager

Young adult

Older adult

Your body is made up of lots of tiny building blocks called **cells.** Different kinds of cells make up different parts of the body. During your childhood, your body makes more and more cells so it will grow and grow and grow!

These are coloured **X-rays** of hands. Notice how big the adult hand is compared to the children's hands.

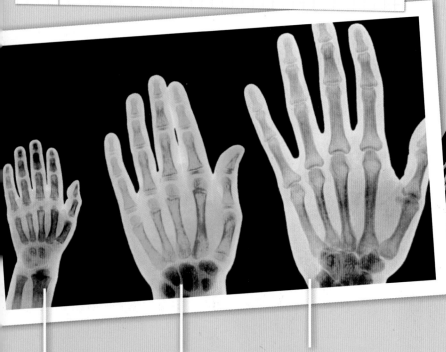

Two-year-old child

Seven-year-old child

Adult

This shows an adult skeleton. As your bones grow longer, you grow taller. How tall you'll be as an adult usually depends on how tall your parents are.

A HEALTHY BODY

Your body needs certain things to help it grow and work properly. Exercise makes your bones and muscles strong, and helps your heart and **lungs** work at their best. Different foods give your body **energy**, help it to grow and repair itself, and protect it from certain illnesses. Sleep gives your body a rest, letting it have a chance to grow.

BRAIN POWER

As your body grows, your brain also learns new things. You take in information through the five senses - seeing, hearing, touching, smelling and tasting. The cells in your brain sort the information so you can remember it. Your brain and your body also learn to work together so you can walk, talk, write your name, ride a bike and do lots of other activities.

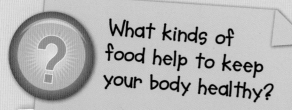

? What kinds of food help to keep your body healthy?

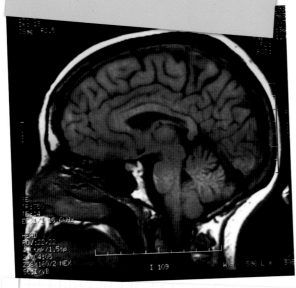

This picture shows the soft, wrinkly surface of a human brain. Your brain grows as you get bigger.

In order to kick a ball, your brain and your body need to work together. Sam's little sister is learning how to do this.

As a baby, you grow and learn more quickly than at any other time in your life. It might seem that a baby doesn't do much, but all the time the baby is taking in new information. That can be tiring!

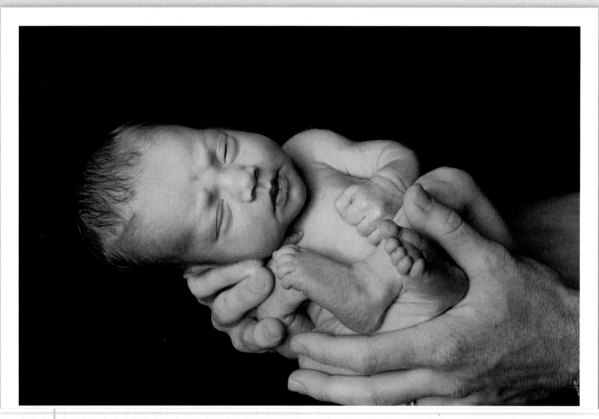

Ivan Andreas is only two days old. He sleeps for about three-quarters of the day. The warmth of his dad's hands is comforting.

NEWBORN BABY

When you were a baby you needed a lot of looking after. You depended on others - probably your parents - for everything. Crying was your main way of telling people what you needed. You cried when you were hungry or cold, or needed a clean nappy.

Maya has learned to move her arms and legs together so she can crawl across the floor.

BASIC SKILLS

As you grew, you learned to do more. You probably gave your first real smile after about six weeks. You made different sounds, such as gurgling and cooing. After about six months, your milk teeth started coming through so you could eat mashed up food.

FIRST YEAR

As you grew older, you became bigger and stronger. Between six months and one year, most babies can sit up and crawl. By your first birthday, you were about three times bigger than when you were born.

Children, especially babies, often learn by copying. Try pulling faces at a baby and see what happens.

By the age of one-and-a-half, most children have learnt to walk. This marks the beginning of the toddler stage. You probably said your first few words at about this age, too. Walking and talking are important **milestones** in growing up.

GROWING AND LEARNING

A toddler's body grows longer, especially compared to the head. As a toddler you learned by playing with adults and older children. You learned about colours, shapes and counting. You may have enjoyed songs and nursery rhymes. Toddlers don't understand about sharing and taking turns. You played alongside other children instead of playing with them.

Saraya has just started walking on her own. Very young children like Saraya are not yet steady on their feet, which is why they're called 'toddlers'.

Lewis and Rory explore the sounds of the bells. They're more interested in the bells than in playing together.

LEARNING CONTROL

Did you have **tantrums** when you were a toddler? Learning to consider other people as well as yourself was the first step towards **controlling** your temper. Learning to talk also meant that you were able to say what you wanted instead of kicking and screaming. Another thing you learned to control was your wee and poo so you could use the toilet. This usually happens at the end of the toddler stage, between the ages of two and three.

Aidan's having a very loud tantrum. He doesn't like learning that he can't have everything he wants.

Toddlers don't know that some things may be dangerous, such as hot kettles or busy roads, so they must be watched carefully and told about the dangers.

As you grew out of the toddler stage at about three years old, you became more aware of the world around you. Young children often ask lots of questions because they are curious about everything.

Jason and his friend, Freya, learn about the world through pretend play.

MAKING FRIENDS

Between the ages of about three and five, you started to think a bit less about yourself and more about other people. You enjoyed playing with other children and started to choose your own friends. You also began to learn that it's kinder to share and take turns.

NEW SKILLS

At this age you were gaining better control of your body. Difficult movements became possible, such as hopping on one leg. Your hands and eyes started working together. Hands and eyes work together for activities such as throwing and catching. Small movements, such as gripping a pencil correctly, became possible as well.

Maryam has learned to hold her pencil correctly. Now it's easier to draw pictures.

Suzanne's eyes, hands and feet have to work together so she can pedal and steer at the same time.

At around three or four years old, children often learn to sing the alphabet, identify letters and learn letter sounds. They are getting ready for reading.

You're probably now in the middle years of childhood - between the ages of about six and twelve. How have you changed? You can do a lot more things than you used to, and you're certainly a lot taller - although you still have more growing to do.

TEETH

Another thing that's changing is your teeth. Your milk teeth are coming out and your adult teeth are coming through. You'll keep these adult teeth for the rest of your life, so look after them!

THINKING FOR YOURSELF

You're now better able to understand right and wrong and you're becoming more **responsible**. You can get yourself ready for school every day and do your chores and homework without being reminded. You might also start thinking into the future, for example, saving your pocket money to buy something special.

Fatima already has some adult teeth. She also has another wobbly milk tooth that will come out soon.

Kiki, Will and their friends meet at the park nearly every Saturday. They like having fun together.

EXPLORING

You're learning to read and write, ride a bike, tie your shoelaces, tell the time - lots of things that you couldn't do before. And you like spending more time with your friends. This is a good age to try new activities and perhaps find a hidden talent or a special hobby to enjoy. Exploring new things makes you feel good about yourself.

Alicia didn't know much about music until she tried playing the guitar. Now she takes lessons and she's even learning the piano too.

How much exercise do you get? Children should exercise for a total of one hour or more every day.

Puberty is the stage of life when your body gets ready to become an adult. You may have a growth spurt and see yourself changing a lot. Your feelings change, too.

Your body will grow taller during puberty. Frank is 15 years old. He's grown 30 centimetres since he was 12.

During puberty, your body works extra hard dealing with all of the changes, so it needs lots of sleep.

HORMONES

Different people start puberty at different ages, but it's usually between the ages of 10 and 14. During puberty, chemicals in your body called **hormones** make lots of changes happen. Girls have female hormones and boys have male hormones. Your hormones will cause hair to grow under your arms and between your legs. You'll also sweat more, so using deodorant under your arms will help you smell fresh.

MOOD SWINGS

Life can seem confusing when you're going through puberty. You're in between being a child and an adult. One minute, you feel happy and lively then you feel down in the dumps. These mood swings are part of the enormous changes that you go through during puberty.

EMOTIONS

As you go through puberty, you may change how you feel about people. You may start thinking about certain people in a **romantic** way. You might even feel like you're falling in love. These feelings are a normal part of becoming an adult.

During puberty, it's common to get spots on your face. Erica tries to keep her skin extra-clean.

Ruby thinks about Marcus all the time, and Marcus gets butterflies in his tummy whenever he's with Ruby.

Girls usually go through puberty at a slightly younger age than boys, but everyone is different. When a girl goes through puberty, it means her body is growing into a woman. Her body grows taller and starts to look curvy, with breasts and rounded hips. She is becoming an adult.

CHANGES

One of the first signs of puberty in a girl is when her breasts begin to grow. Then the parts of her body that will make it possible for her to have a baby, called the **reproductive system**, start getting ready to do their job. Every month, hormones cause her ovaries to release a tiny egg into her tubes. The egg moves through her tubes to her **womb**.

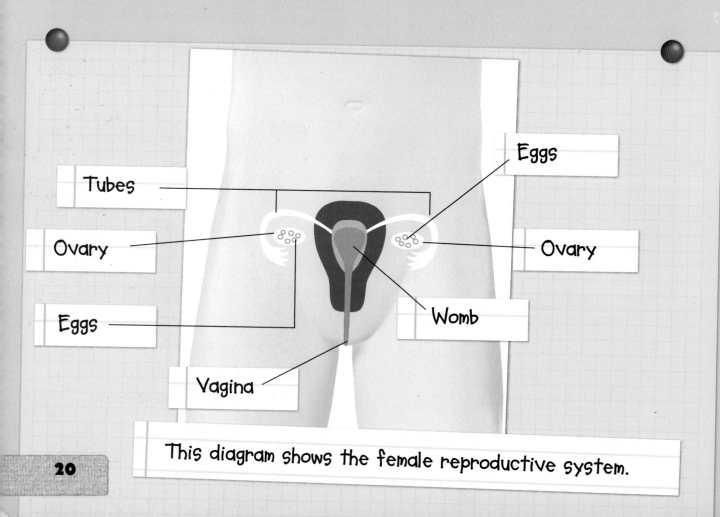

Tubes

Ovary

Eggs

Vagina

Eggs

Ovary

Womb

This diagram shows the female reproductive system.

MONTHLY PERIOD

Usually, the tiny egg, along with the lining of the womb, comes out as blood through her **vagina**. The blood lasts for a few days and is called her monthly **period**. A pregnant woman won't get her monthly period because the egg stays in the womb and grows into a baby.

Special pads called sanitary towels soak up the blood when you have your period. No one will know that it's your time of the month.

Hayley and her friends are teenagers – in between being children and adults. Even though it's possible for Hayley to make a baby now, she knows that she's not ready to be a mum.

When a boy goes through puberty, it means his body is growing into a man. His body grows taller, with more muscle. He is becoming an adult.

CHANGES

During puberty, a boy's shoulders and chest get wider. He starts growing hair on his chest, underarms and between his legs. On his face, he starts growing whiskers, which he may want to shave off.

During puberty, a boy's voice box grows, making his voice deeper. The voice box can be seen as a large bump in the neck, called the Adam's apple.

Kwame and his friends are starting to grow a few whiskers, but it will be a few more years before they grow enough whiskers for a beard.

MAKING SPERM

The male reproductive system has a penis, also known as a willy, and two testicles, also known as balls. The testicles are inside a bag of skin called the scrotum. During puberty, a boy's hormones cause his testicles to start making millions and millions of sperm. When millions of tiny sperm flow from the testicles and out through the penis, it is called an **ejaculation**. Only one sperm is needed to make a baby.

A.J. is a teenager – in between being a child and an adult. Even though it's possible for A.J. to make a baby now, he knows that he's not ready to be a dad.

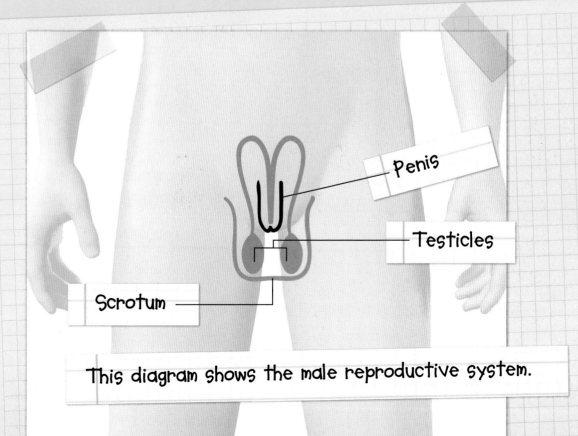

Penis

Testicles

Scrotum

This diagram shows the male reproductive system.

You will become an adult when your body stops growing, probably between the ages of 18 and 20. But there's more to being an adult than that.

CHOICES

Being an adult means making big choices. Where will you live? Will you travel? What kind of job will you have? You'll have to decide what's right for you and sometimes you'll make mistakes. But life is about learning, even for adults.

RESPONSIBILITIES

Along with choices there are **responsibilities**. You'll need to work to pay for things such as a place to live. Like children, adults also need plenty of exercise and sleep, and need to eat well. Behaving like an adult means being sensible, while still having fun! Sometimes, adults find this hard to do.

What do you think you'll do when you're an adult? Will you be a plumber, a doctor or a teacher? Or will you travel the world? The choices are endless.

Being a parent is lots of fun, but it's not easy.

HAVING CHILDREN

Being a mum or dad is the biggest responsibility there is. Your children will depend on you and it will be your job to care for them until they are able to care for themselves.

END OF LIFE

As you get older and older, your hair will turn grey and your skin will get wrinkly. Parts of your body will start to wear out. By trying to keep active, people can often enjoy old age. However, everyone must die sometime. People die and others are born - that is the human life cycle.

Irene is 78 years old and still likes to have fun!

How you look on the outside is just one small part of who you are. It's what's on the inside that makes you truly special - your personality, what you like (and don't like!), your skills and talents and the things that are important to you.

Anthony, Omar and Becky think it's important to help the environment, and they want to do something about it.

? What's important to you? Family? Friends? School? Hobbies? Your future?

LEARNING ALL THE TIME

As you grow up, you'll have the chance to try new things and discover more about yourself. Your body may stop getting taller when you become an adult, but you never stop growing as a person. Your brain continues to develop and learn all through your life. So you're always changing, even if those changes can't always be seen.

Abby and her friends may not be pop stars, but they're all special people.

YOUR LIFE

Although you've grown up a lot since you were a baby, you're still near the beginning of your life cycle. You've got most of your life ahead of you. You have lots of choices to make, and you also have responsibilities. Remember - your life is special. Enjoy it!

? What are some of the special things that make you, you?

Adult a fully grown person

Cell a tiny unit that together with other cells makes up a living thing

Control to have power over something in order to deal with it

Ejaculation when sperm flows out of the penis

Energy the power to carry out activities

Hormones a natural chemical made by the body which triggers a reaction. During puberty, hormones trigger development of the reproductive system

Human being a person

Life cycle changes that happen throughout life

Lungs the organs that humans and other animals use for breathing

Milestones important stages in growing up

Period the regular (usually monthly) flow of blood experienced by girls and women after puberty

Personality a set of qualities that make one person different from another

Puberty a stage of the life cycle in which a person begins to grow into an adult

Reproductive system the parts of the body that make it possible to have a baby

Responsibilities things that a person is trusted to look after

Responsible sensible and mature, able to be trusted

Romantic having to do with love

Tantrum showing bad temper, often by kicking and screaming

Unique the only one of its kind

Vagina a passage that leads to the womb in girls and women

Womb an organ that a woman has where babies can grow before birth

X-ray a kind of photograph of the inside of the body

Websites

Change 4 Life - Eat well, move more, live longer
www.nhs.uk/change4life/Pages/Make.aspx

Food Standards Agency - Eat well, be well. Helping you make healthier choices
www.eatwell.gov.uk

Kids health - A US website with information for older children about growing up and puberty.
http://kidshealth.org/kid/grow/index.html

Note to parents and teachers: Every effort has been made by the Publishers to ensure that these websites are suitable for children, that they are of the highest educational value, and that they contain no inappropriate or offensive material. However, because of the nature of the Internet, it is impossible to guarantee that the contents of these sites will not be altered. We strongly advise that Internet access is supervised by a responsible adult.

Books

How Will I Grow? by Mick Manning and Brita Granstrom (Franklin Watts)

What Makes Me, Me? by Dr Robert Winston (Dorling Kindersley)

Hair, There and Everywhere: A Book About Growing Up by Jacqui Bailey (Franklin Watts)

Hair in Funny Places by Babette Cole (Red Fox)

Your Body Inside and Out: Growing by Andrew Solway (Franklin Watts)

Usborne Internet-linked First Encyclopedia of the Human Body by Fiona Chandler (Usborne Children's Books)

INDEX

adults 6, 7, 8, 12, 16, 18, 19, 20, 21, 22, 23, 24-27

babies 6, 10, 11, 20, 21, 23, 27
bones 8, 9
brain 9, 26

cells 8, 9
children 6, 8, 11, 12, 14, 15, 17, 19, 21, 23, 24, 25

death 6, 25

exercise 9, 17, 24

feelings 18, 19
friends 14, 17, 21, 22, 27

growth spurts 18

hair 18, 22, 25
hobbies 17
hormones 18, 20, 23

learning 9, 10, 11, 12, 13, 15, 17, 24, 26

life cycle 6, 25, 27
life expectancy 7

making choices 24, 27
movement 9, 11, 12, 14, 15, 17
muscles 9, 22

period 21
personality 7, 26
playing 12, 13, 14
puberty 18-23

reading 15, 17
reproductive system 20, 23
responsibilities 24, 25, 27

skeleton 8
sleep 9, 10, 18, 24

talking 9, 12, 13
tantrums 13
teenagers 7, 18-23
teeth 11, 16
toddlers 6, 12, 13, 14

walking 9